PREACHING UNDER THE INFLUENCE

A Minister's Struggle

PREACHING UNDER THE INFLUENCE
A Minister's Struggle

BRANDON HOLT

purposely created PUBLISHING

PREACHING UNDER THE INFLUENCE
Published by Purposely Created Publishing Group™

Copyright © 2018 Brandon Holt

All rights reserved.

Scriptures marked NKJV are taken from the New King James Version®. Copyright © 1982 by Thomas Nelson. All rights reserved.

Printed in the United States of America

ISBN: 978-1-948400-53-4

Special discounts are available on bulk quantity purchases by book clubs, associations and special interest groups. For details email: sales@publishyourgift.com or call (888) 949-6228.

For information log on to www.PublishYourGift.com

DEDICATION

———— ◆ ————

I want to dedicate this book to anyone directly or indirectly who has struggled or continues to struggle with substance use disorders or mental health disorders.

This book is also dedicated to everyone who has lost his or her life to substance use disorders and mental health disorders, and to all of the men and women who are incarcerated, particularly when drugs were associated with their crimes.

To the hopeless, and to those who have given up on themselves, this one is for you, too.

TABLE OF CONTENTS

ACKNOWLEDGMENTS

I would like to acknowledge my wife, Crystal, our three sons (Brandon Jr., Caleb, Mason) and our daughter, Harper. They stood in the gap with me when I could not stand alone.

Thank you to my mother and father, Muriel and Carlton Holt, for their unconditional love and support throughout every step of the journey.

I am grateful for my mother-in-law and father-in-law, Myra and Michael Anderson, for their undying love and kindness towards my family.

I am indebted to my brothers, CJ and Dave, for always challenging me to strive for greatness and success.

I would like to thank Mikki Taylor, my creative director, for conceptualizing and directing an extraordinary cover shoot.

Thank you to my photographer, Jay Clark, who captured one dynamic image after another.

Thank you to my groomer, Koda McDowell, who made sure I was polished to perfection!

Thank you to Connie "Bodacious" Williams, my photo shoot coordinator, who graciously pulled everything together.

And special thanks to Minister OJ Heyward, Dr. Ron Stewart, and Judge Hazel Jones for their masterful words on *Preaching Under the Influence: A Minister's Struggle.*

I extend warm gratitude to my first counseling directors and mentors, Ms. Carol Nunn and Ms. Toby Bradley, for bringing me into the helping field, training me, and teaching me everything I now know.

Thank you to my friend, brother, and mentor, Terrell Williams, for teaching me the importance of humility and thankfulness.

To Minister Tim Daniels of the Trinity Gardens Church of Christ: thank you for serving as my ministerial coach and accountability partner.

To my comrade, Jimmy Hurd, I'm appreciative of your teaching me the value of true friendship.

Thank you to my uncle, Robert Holt, for providing a shoulder to lean on during my most difficult days.

I am endlessly grateful for the church leaders, secretaries, and parishioners I have worked with over the years for believing in me.

An eternal thank you to my late grandfather, G.P. Holt, for introducing me to the pulpit. If I could have one more conversation with him now, I would just hug him and simply say thank you.

To my church family, the Connect Church of Christ in Baytown, Texas: thank you for helping me plant the congregation and entrusting me as your leader.

I extend a unique thank you to my friend, Andre Gray, for hiring me to cut hair at his First Place Barbershop in 2009. Some of the greatest men I have ever met worked there as barbers, and they each gave me an opportunity to rebuild and regain hope.

I'm eternally grateful for my first grade Bible class teacher, Ms. Doris Green, for rewarding me with Charms Blow Pop candies whenever I successfully memorized a scripture.

Thank you to my childhood minister, John Cannon, who has been very inspirational to me over the years.

I want to extend a huge thank you to our family counselor in California, Jessie Trice, who supported my wife and me during our difficult times and helped us see past the challenges and find our way back into one another's hearts. If it were not for him, I do not know where we would be.

And, to all of my family and everyone else who has been there for me: thank you.

FOREWORD

True freedom lies within us all. Allowing God to guide us down that path is our choice and ours alone. In this text, Brandon depicts a provocative and heart-wrenching story of how he was challenged with several obstacles in his life, yet God placed people in his path that led him to a life of redemption. Alcohol and drugs destroy so many lives. The many people who are connected to the abuser experience some type of destruction as well. Restoring those lives will take time. Brandon shares how he allowed God to work with him, to reach out to others, to own his truth, and to become the man he is today. The words in this text will inspire many. No matter what your profession or background is, you can find comfort in knowing that God walks with us through our darkest moments. Through his Faith, Courage, and his belief in Almighty God, Brandon beat the odds and lived to tell his story.

Carol J. Nunn
LPCI, ASOTP, LCDC, CCJP, MA

INTRODUCTION

---◆---

In some capacity, we are all going through life, juggling responsibilities and balancing our hats as fathers, husbands, brothers, sons, and friends. We are all doing our best not to drop a single task while simultaneously making it look clean and effortless. As the saying goes, "Never let them see you sweat." The goal is to find rhythm and reach our potential until we have successfully accomplished our unique life's calling. For the purpose of growing and expanding, we continuously add layers to situations that are sometimes already hard to balance. At least, that was the case for me. Then, I dropped the most important asset I had.

I lost my family.

* * *

Ten years ago, I traveled four hours away to serve as a guest speaker in Fresno, California. On my way home from this conference, my wife called and said that she had left me and California for good. My ego refused to believe her. She wasn't gone—she was just threatening me again. In my spirit, however, I knew the truth. When I got home, sure enough, everything was gone.

1

She had left a note on the bathroom counter saying she had taken the kids and moved back to Texas. I immediately called one of the leaders of my church home to tell him what had happened and hopefully to receive guidance. Instead, he gave me an opportunity to resign with dignity, while immediately dismissing me from my position as senior minister due to not fulfilling my responsibilities as a husband.

At that point, all I wanted to do was move back to Texas—where both my wife and I are from—to reunite with my family and try to put all the pieces of my broken puzzle back together. I had to get back to them. I attempted to make a short sale on our house, but it did not work out. The home that we had once prayed for and celebrated went into foreclosure. It was almost as if all the balls that I had been juggling, one by one, had all started falling and shattering right in front of me. My beautiful family was gone. My career was gone. My identity was gone. My self-esteem was gone. My pride was shot.

All of my life, I had successfully managed everything that was put before me. As a kid, I played basketball, baseball, golf, soccer, and football while simultaneously making sure my grades didn't slip. I also completed chores around the house, helping my family in any way that I could. By the time I was 16 years old, I was playing sports, dating, and preaching. Following my high school graduation, my interest in athletics was replaced by my college classes and my barbering practices. I was still dating and preaching, and by the age of 24, I was married and had just welcomed our first son into the world. I had been given the opportunity of a lifetime: we moved from Arlington, Texas to Southern California so that I could preach the word of God with the additional perk of a pretty handsome salary.

Since I'd lost everything, I felt like the Lord had abandoned me. I felt that He'd walked away from me because I failed to complete the ministry assignment which was ministering to my family first and foremost. I did not claim to be perfect (never had), but I still could not understand what was happening or why. I had had it all then lost it all in what felt like a matter of just seconds. The only things I had left were my own life and my addiction to Codeine and Vicodin; they could relax every nerve in my body by releasing enough dopamine from my brain to make me feel confident and clever enough to survive any situation. Whenever the euphoric high lapsed and the reality of life set in, I was always one swallow away from being in control again. Ironically, the very presence in my life that made me lose everything was also the only staple that I could rely on in those moments.

When I moved back to Texas, I was in survival mode spiritually, mentally, and financially. If anyone has ever experienced this, you can relate to how stressful that life station is. I was geographically closer to my family, but my wife and I were still separated. My opioid use disorder had become so bad that I was red-flagged in Dallas for "doctor shopping," meaning I was going around to different doctor's offices and medical facilities in search of a licensed provider who would prescribe me Codeine or Vicodin. I started buying opioid painkillers from acquaintances to help counter the symptoms of withdrawal. One day, my five-year-old son BJ called and asked when I was coming home. His phone call triggered something in me; it was my wake-up call. At that very moment, I knew something had to change.

BEFORE THE OPIOID USE DISORDER

———◆———

"Trust in the Lord with all your heart, And lean not on your own understanding; In all your ways acknowledge Him, And He shall direct your paths."

—Proverbs 3:5-6 (NKJV)

Growing Up

I grew up with both parents in the household, and they loved each other dearly. I was the youngest child with two older brothers. We had a warm home, full of love. Holidays, birthdays, and vacations were big deals in our family, and we placed great emphasis on enjoying our time together. My father, Carlton, was a salesman while my mother, Muriel, worked for American Airlines as a flight service manager. Her position allowed us the opportunity to fly all over the world for vacations to places such as Hawaii, Canada, Mexico, Puerto Rico, and Jamaica. You could say that I had it made, maybe even spoiled. However, I still had plenty of discipline and structure.

Independence and responsibility were core values in our house. Like every other kid around me, I grew up with chores; I had to do yard work and help clean up around the house, which taught me the value of a dollar. I was provided the basic necessities, but if I wanted the latest Michael Jordan sneakers, I had to come up with half the money—my parents would help with the other half. We were taught good work ethics, too—how to get a job, how to keep a job, and how to survive in the world on our own. I recall first working at the local grocery store as a young teenager, making four dollars and twenty-five cents an hour, stocking produce and anxiously awaiting every paycheck.

Like most kids, I did not always see how blessed I was. I remember running away from home one time—or at least attempting to. I was about 16 or 17 years old, and I remember that I didn't get my way about something or another. I told my parents I was running away, and they didn't try to stop me. While furiously packing my belongings, I remember my father saying, "Where are you going with my things?" I saw his point but still wanted to stand my ground, so I left the house with only the clothes on my back. I went as far as the corner of the street and sat down on the curb for a few minutes before realizing I didn't have anywhere to go. I went back home and apologized for not realizing how great I had it.

Integrity was another principle my parents lived by: do the right thing when no one is looking. My parents were very friendly to everyone they met; they respected each other, attended church faithfully, and prayed before every meal. To this day, I have never even heard my father utter a curse word, though I realize, of course, that doesn't mean he never did. I, however, had a hard time showing care and compassion because I had an anger problem. I didn't always treat people right, but whenever I see someone who I mistreated in the past, I make a point to acknowledge what I did and attempt to make amends.

The root of my anger stemmed from how I was treated for being biracial. White people called me a "nigger" and black people called me a "cracker." I was too dark for my white friends and too light for my black friends. I was lost, confused, and just trying to fit in. Every day, I asked the question "what color am I?" I recall a Latino friend saying "Holt, just get down with the brown." I never really felt accepted by most people; as a result, there was a lot of shame around who I was and who my parents were. During elementary school, I fit in more with white kids, which made me closer to my mom since she was white; this also meant that I would get teased whenever my dad, a black man came around. I also only dated white girls—even my first kiss was with a white girl in first grade. She lived on my street, and we went to the same school. We were walking down the hallway one day, and my friend and I took turns kissing her. It was just a peck on the cheek, but I was *sprung*. She moved away when we were going into the second grade, and it broke my young heart.

By the time I reached high school, though, the way I identified myself flipped. I started identifying more with black kids, and I also started dating black girls. Instead of being teased about my dad, the teasing was then about my mom. In the '80s, interracial relationships were still not as widely accepted as they are now, so I can only imagine what my parents experienced in the '60s and '70s. My mom is originally from Sac City, Iowa, a small county town of a few thousand white people. I remember visiting Sac City once when I was 14 years old, and kids thought my brother and I were so

9

cool, most likely because they had probably never seen black kids. My dad is originally from the inner city of Indianapolis, Indiana, where the majority of the residents were black, quite the opposite of Sac City.

Both of my parents moved to Arlington, Texas as adults. My father was coaching basketball at Southwestern Christian College, and my mother was attending Abilene Christian University to teach education. They met through a mutual friend, who they remain friends with today. They started dating, and the rest is history. A few years later, they got married, started a family, and demonstrated one of the most beautiful versions of love that I have ever witnessed—then and now. I did not resent my parents or their union at all; I was bitter because I felt as though I didn't fit in; I was tired of being asked what color I was. I was sick of being called "Oreo" and "Zebra." More than anything, I hated being asked what I was, as if I wasn't human at all. Eventually, I reached a point of clarity where I believed God must have spent some extra time when creating me, and I learned not only to accept that I came from two different worlds, but I learned to be thankful for it. I was lucky enough to experience black and white cultures. Before I came to that realization, however, I still resented my background and demonstrated a lot of anger because of it.

While I was in high school, I channeled most of that anger through sports and played basketball and football. Basketball, however, was really my passion. For the longest time, I dreamed of being one of the 0.03 percent of high school basketball players who would make it to the NBA. But then, during my senior year at Arlington Bowie High School, I dislocated my shoulder and had to switch gears. Instead of playing professional ball, I accepted the practical reality that instead, I would cut hair. It wasn't a career path that I picked out of thin air; my parents were adamant about teaching us how to survive, and it was a skill that would help me do just that. And, in this world, you can't always place your bets on just one plan; you need a plan B, C, and D.

My dad explained that establishing a trade would provide me with a solid backup plan. I developed a love for cutting hair in high school, watching my cousins perfect the craft. I practiced on my own hair, my brothers', and whoever else would allow me the opportunity to practice on them. My brothers thought it was really cool, and it certainly beat having to go to the barber shop all the time. Since I was still learning and growing, I messed up quite a bit. I recall many arguments with my brother CJ for pushing his edge back too far. That's when I decided it would help to enhance my focus and attend the renowned Williams Barber College, located in Fort Worth, Texas in 1998 at 19 years old.

After completing 1,500 hours of training, I took the final exam in Austin, Texas. There was a written component and a demonstration—a haircut and a shave. I passed the written part with flying colors, but I barely made it through the demonstration; I laid my dad back for the hot lather shave, and my nerves kicked in: I slit him right on the cheek with the razor, and he immediately started gushing blood. Luckily the exam evaluators were not physically over on that side to see what happened, so I was able to put some talcum powder on the cut quickly and finish. My dad was fuming, but I managed to clean it up expeditiously. By the time the evaluators came around to my chair, they didn't notice a thing. I passed.

Besides playing sports and cutting hair, girls also had my full attention; I was a ladies man, and I had multiple girlfriends at any given time. Despite this, I was still trying to hold onto my virginity since I entered the ministry around this time, but it got harder and harder to resist the urge. While still in high school at the age of 16, I preached my first sermon at the Wilmer Hutchins Church. I preached on Sundays, making a little money. I owe my late grandfather, G.P. Holt, Sr. and uncle, Robert L. Holt, Sr. for training me to preach at such a young age. Whenever my grandfather preached at a church either out of town or locally, he allowed me to get two or three minutes in—just enough time for a hallelujah shout. I loved it!

Preaching was in my blood, and at a young age, it was already in me. For years throughout my childhood and adolescence, I had silently observed, envisioned, practiced, and trained while my grandfather and uncle preached. I eventually realized that being a preacher was not what I *did*—it was who I *was* and who I *am* today. I eventually earned my grandfather's blessing to preach. He challenged me to memorize Acts 2:1-47, the whole chapter, which took me a couple of months. Once I memorized it, I was tasked to then quote it in front of him. In retrospect, I realize that it was less about quoting that chapter and more about training my mind to quote scripture and really learn how to retain them in my memory so that I wouldn't depend on manuscripts every time I preached.

After I passed the test of memorization, my grandfather helped me arrange my first sermon. One of his best friends, J.S. Winston, the senior minister of Wilmer Hutchins Church, opened the pulpit for me. I was nervous all day leading up to the sermon, but I refused to allow my fears to deter me. I walked out and mounted the pulpit in my long, yellow suit, with my six pages of notes in hand, scared to death, wondering if I had forgotten something and if my sermon would come out right. *What if they don't say amen?* The audience looked at me like, "Who is this young dude?" I was shaking with nerves, but as soon as my mouth opened, I came into my new element, and the fear disappeared.

The title of my first sermon was "Out of Bounds." You know when preachers have other people read a scripture for them? The preacher might say, "Read for me 1 Peter Chapter 2 Verse 1." The other person then reads it, and then the preacher repeats the words and what is to be emphasized. I thought it was a cool thing to do, so I looked over to Minister Winston and my grandfather, two legends in the front row listening to me *try* to preach, and I said, "Winston, read for me the next two verses." I was disciplined when I was done.

My grandfather scolded me with, "Don't you ever call an older preacher by his last name like that. You *always* say brother in front of it." That lesson taught me, not necessarily to say brother to an elderly man, but it taught me to always acknowledge someone you know as Mr. or Mrs. or Brother or Sister, especially someone of an older age. It was a lesson in respect.

I preached my second sermon at the church I grew up in—the Pleasant Ridge Church. My parents have been members there for over 30 years and still attend to this day. It was a predominantly Caucasian church, so I switched my style to match the church's style. In African-American churches, you hear a lot of "Amen!" and emotional singing and so forth. In predominantly white churches, however, I had more of a quiet and reserved audience. Since I grew up in a predominantly white church for the first 15 years of my life, I was more accustomed to the lecture-style of preaching versus the elevated voice and scream-and-sweat style, which aims to make the congregation *feel* it and become emotionally charged while hearing the Word of God.

I was clearly not a stranger to multiple styles of sermon delivery. While I was blessed to experience both cultures as a teenager, I eventually found myself gravitated more towards the African-American culture and church because at the time I felt that I fit in more there. In the multicultural church, I dealt with many of the same people who had the same struggles that I did growing up—too dark to be white and too white to be black. Once I started preaching, I began asking myself how I could use my biracial upbringing to advance the gospel of Jesus Christ. My vision was to always cultivate and grow a diverse, multicultural church; I felt that was a reflection of me and the united diversity that I wanted to see more of throughout the world.

I had not yet discovered my authentic voice, though. Many artists and athletes admit that when they first started perfecting their crafts, they were simply imitating the styles of their role models. The same went for me. Until I began to find my own rhythm and approach to preaching, I parodied other preachers, my grandfather especially. I thought it was impressive to preach loudly, slapping the Bible on the podium while quoting a lot of scriptures. Watching the people in the audience get wound up never ceased to be exciting.

Eventually, more churches—local and national—started inviting me to preach. With my mother's American Airlines benefits, I could use her plane tickets to cover the travel expenses if the host congregation could not finance the trip. I was getting opportunities all over the country to preach, and I would flirt with the young ladies while I was in their respective cities. I had a girlfriend back home, but that didn't stop me from kissing hands and taking phone numbers. I dated as much as I could before marriage to make sure I found my soulmate. I remember dating a young lady in Atlanta, another in California, one in Seattle, and two in Dallas; I ended up falling in love—what I thought was love—with all five.

My dad once said, "You will know when the right one comes, without question." That undoubtable knowing, which was one of the best days of my life, came while serving as a guest preacher in Harlem, New York in 1997. While serving my sermon, I immediately locked eyes with Crystal Anderson from Dallas, Texas. I can still very clearly recall her sexy smile, silky caramel skin, glowing hair, diamond earrings, pink dress, black high heels, and transition-tinted glasses. I was "outta there," sprung and in love—right in the middle of explaining the text from the pulpit.

We couldn't stop looking at each other, blushing, smiling, and anticipating the first introduction. I fumbled through the sermon as I would catch an occasional smile from her. She was the wife of my dreams, and this experience I was having from across the room was different. I immediately recalled my dad's words: *"You will immediately know when you've met the one."* I felt as though God sent her there just for me. We were both about 17 or 18 at the time. When the Harlem Church announced the visitors, I learned that she was in town for an NAACP singing competition, and later I found out that we only lived about 30 minutes from each other back in Texas. While shaking her hand after the

17

service, I felt like kissing her on the spot, but I knew better. This was special, and I couldn't and didn't want to mess this up. I got her number and called immediately from my parents' home phone upon returning. Our first conversation was very nerve-racking; we kept asking each other the same questions and fumbling over our words.

We kept in touch during high school and continued to talk after graduation. We both decided to attend Southwestern Christian College, which was founded by my great-great grandfather, George P. Bowser. He originally set its location in a small town called Silver Point, Tennessee and later moved the college to Terrell, Texas about 30 minutes east of Dallas. Crystal and I weren't together yet, but when we got to college, however, she wanted to establish a serious relationship with me. Even though I knew she was the one, I still wasn't interested in committing to a serious relationship just yet; I wanted to meet the other girls on campus and date around to see what else was out there. It was my freshman year, and I was hesitant to get tied down to one woman at such a young age.

Eventually, she got a boyfriend, and I got a girlfriend; I stayed with this girl for about two years and actually ended up proposing to her. Crystal and I continued to stay in touch with each other throughout the years and somehow managed to still stay in love from a distance. She always remained close to my heart; the love was always there, but we never crossed the boundaries. I remember one time when she went out of town with the school chorus for 14 days, and even though we weren't together yet, I still wrote 14 letters and mailed them all to her at the same time with instructions to read one letter per day. I later found out that she was so excited, she read them all at once!

I knew we were destined to be together, and I finally realized I didn't want to stall anymore. We split from our partners and finally decided to officially solidify our love without looking back. It felt like a dream come true. She was just as beautiful inside as she was on the outside, and I didn't have to talk to her to know it—I felt it from the moment we locked eyes in Harlem, and getting to know her only confirmed it. She was the love of my life. I couldn't think of anyone else more perfect for me—she was attractive, smart, a great cook, nurturing, could sing like an angel, and she was a woman of God. I often told her, "I didn't know angels flew so low." When the time would come for me to become a senior minister, she would be right by my side.

I grew up in the church, went to Bible study, and participated in youth camps, so when it came time for college, I decided to pursue a degree in ministry. I earned my barbering license at 19, but I also knew that was just my backup plan—preaching for a church was my primary goal. I played basketball for the college in addition to studying ministry. In retrospect, I was too young and immature to be preaching; my heart was in it, but I had not yet expunged the womanizing lifestyle out of my system despite my budding relationship with Crystal. I was still too curious and too big of a thrill-seeker. The same pull that I felt with girls in high school followed me into college as well; by now, I was both the preacher and the athlete. The ladies loved that duality about me, and I practiced little self-control in the face of that temptation.

If I could go back and have a talk with the me back then, I probably still would not have stepped down from the pulpit. Christianity was my life, and even now, I can't think of anything more empowering than the gospel. Studying the Word of God adds another level of enlightenment, and then there's preaching it— standing before the congregation, who's just as hungry for the Word as you are, is both freeing and exciting. Being the center of attention, of course, doesn't hurt either.

When you're up on the podium, it's all eyes on you; everyone is locked in to you. While being center stage is some people's fear, it was my fuel. For 25 to 30 minutes, all eyes were on me, which triggered an approval addiction. I was naturally charismatic, so people were naturally drawn to me. On top of that, the congregation would constantly tell me how much they loved my sermon, creating a need for validation. That attention plus the need for approval turned the pulpit into my place of solace. I'd gone from not being accepted to being the one everyone wanted to be around—both in church and in school.

College was a dream. Beyond the typical routine of going to class, mingling with classmates, stuffing my face with pizza, and dating, I also traveled a lot all over the country since I was playing guard for the basketball team. While I still had my mother's flight benefits, I traveled on weekends to preach and make a little extra money on the side. I was a superstar, having the time of my life. I had my cake, and I ate it, too—every bit of it.

It was also in college when I was introduced to sleep aids for the first time. I noticed that a friend of mine could fall asleep at the snap of a finger and be knocked out cold, whereas I had trouble falling asleep at all. I asked him one day how he did it, and he handed me a few pills. They were over-the-counter Advil PM pills, so I didn't see anything glaringly wrong with it. I tried a dose one night, and it worked; just like him, I could be knocked out almost instantly. Whenever I wanted to go to sleep, I no longer had to lay awake for hours, waiting for my brain to shut down. All it took was a pill, and I'd start snoring.

Everything seemed to be going my way. From the outside looking in, it was like I was in control of everything in my life and was incapable of losing. Some people called it a *god complex*; my ego felt that I could do no wrong and that I was unstoppable. I was 21 years old and on top of the world. Even though the NBA wasn't my dream anymore, I still had basketball as a hobby. I had my barbering license to fall back on just in case. Crystal had become my girlfriend and eventually my wife; it was divine timing. I had always been in love with her, but at this point, I was head-over-heels in love. I always wanted to be around her, and if I wasn't with her in person, we were on the phone. Not long after we got married, I received a phone call from Southern California with an invitation to become the Senior Minister at a church in the city of Corona.

It was as if life was whispering, "On your mark. Get set. Go!" Since I'm competitive by nature and always have been, when the whistle blew, I was gone!

Settling Down and Leveling Up

When Crystal and I were engaged, we became pregnant with our first son, which was difficult for many reasons. People assumed that we were only getting married because of the baby on the way, and even though we knew that was not the reason, it still hurt. Additionally, I was a preacher, so it looked terrible; as a man and woman of God, we were supposed to wait until we exchanged vows before we knew each other in that way, but simply put, we didn't. Then, on top of that, I had been given the opportunity to preach for my first church in California. I was concerned about their acceptance of me if they knew about our pregnancy out of wedlock.

I wanted everything to be out in the open, so I called the church and let them know that I had gotten my fiancée pregnant before our wedding ceremony. I recognized that I could have covered it up for a short period of time, but I didn't want to. I wanted to start and maintain a clean slate. I made the decision to be transparent at the last minute due to fear of the unknown. When I made the phone call to the church leaders, we were outside of my wife's parents' house near the U-Haul with everything loaded up, preparing for our relocation to California. "Hey, my fiancée is pregnant. I just want you all to know. If you do not want me, I completely understand. Trust me, I get it."

Luckily, they accepted us with open arms, and I am eternally grateful for it.

Crystal and I were off to a world of new beginnings: a pending marriage, a new state, a new job, and a baby on the way.

We started off on our new journey excited and anxious to see all that was in store for us as a young, soon-to-be-married couple, branching away and starting fresh, and it started off great! We would take weekly weekend adventures to Hollywood, Beverly Hills, San Diego, and Los Angeles, shopping, sampling restaurants, visiting beaches, and just familiarizing ourselves with our new environment. It was expensive to live in this area, but the church took care of us providing a wonderful salary with great benefits. It was an ideal lifestyle. Eventually the newness wore off and reality set in with all its challenges. One of the first things we realized was that we didn't get a chance to know each other as husband and wife *before* becoming parents; we had a baby on the way going into the wedding and into a new environment a great distance from Texas.

Leading up to our son's birth, I was excited but also terrified: I didn't have a clue what it would take to raise a child. My father did a masterful job with my brothers and me, but being a child and becoming a father are wildly different experiences. I realized that it was more of a fear of the unknown; we were comfortable with what we knew. Whenever there's a transition into the unknown, of course, there's going to be inevitable nerves and a little hesitancy. Would I be a good father? What do I do? Both of our parents lived in Texas, and we were about to have another life in our hands. How is that going to work?

The day of my son's birth is one I'll never forget. The umbilical cord was wrapped around his neck, so Crystal had to have an emergency Caesarean section, making the ordeal even more terrifying. This experience, however, demonstrated the fragility of life and how blessed we all are to have it. After a terrifying delivery, our son was born—we named him Brandon Donald Holt, Jr. Not only was I now someone's father, but I was also a senior, something I never knew I valued until the day I saw his face. My heart was humbled to see our baby with my namesake. As brand new parents, we did the best we could, and we made it work. After a while, however, the struggles set in; it wasn't peaceful adjusting to all the changes around and within us, and there was little downtime for either of us to simply sit and process or reflect on anything. We were in constant go-mode. Our lives, which was once all about each other and our dreams, now revolved around this beautiful little human being who depended on us for everything.

Furthermore, I wanted to make sure my new role at the congregation was a success. I still remember my first day there in the pulpit; I horrifically blanked and forgot everything I learned in preaching school. Since I was accustomed to preaching in churches with predominantly black congregations, I didn't know if I should talk loudly or lecture in this one since it was mixed (white, black, and Latino). I had yet to discover my personal style, and this lack of identity was more evident than ever. It reminded me of growing up biracial, not knowing how to identify myself. It was my dream, however, to minister before a mixed audience, but alas, there I was, clueless. My first 15 or so sermons were from previous lessons over the years, yet I was committed to finding my footing and mastering my role.

Unfortunately, during this process of finding my professional style and voice, I ended up neglecting my family. I was mentally and physically exhausted. Crystal and I were both tired with very little time or energy to cater to anything besides paying bills, taking care of things around the house, and raising our son. It takes two people to tango, but I knew I was letting my partner down on a daily basis. She was a great wife, a great mother, and a strong woman. Instead of leveraging that, however, I leaned on it instead. I took advantage of her and practically left her to do it all alone. Physically I was there, but rarely was I ever mentally or emotionally present.

Two years later, our second son, Caleb, was born. It was a little less turbulent simply because we somewhat knew what to expect, and the Caesarean was scheduled, so there was less guessing and worrying about the delivery. It wasn't until Caleb was born that I realized that we had only just gotten somewhat used to being parents and balancing the responsibilities with Brandon, Jr. Everyone talks about how difficult it is for a firstborn child to suddenly have to share the attention of his parents with a new baby, but it's also a huge adjustment for the parents. We had to learn how to divide our focus and energy again, meaning even less time with one another as a couple.

The adjustment was hard, especially on my wife, because the majority of my attention was still in the church. A lot of our disagreements were due to me putting the congregation before my family; I was always gone, always ministering to somebody, and always wanting to impress the leaders. My absence was a big contributor to our arguments because before moving to California, we never had many arguments. Adding to the stress and discord of being new parents to two young children, I became a substance user.

OPIOID USE DISORDER

Like Michelangelo said best, "I saw the angel in a marble and carved until I set him free." I, too, was that angel trapped in the marble of drug abuse with no hope of getting out. Through the pain, humiliation, and embarrassment, I realize God was setting me free.

How It Got Started

In 2005, about two to three years after accepting my role as Senior Minister, I got into a serious car accident while on the way to a church camp retreat in Big Bear, California. I was driving up a hill at about 45 miles per hour when the car in front of me stopped suddenly. Before I could swerve or slam on my breaks, I crashed into the back of the car. Upon impact, I felt a mighty muscle jerk in my lower backbone. I immediately knew that something was wrong, yet I refused to be transported by the ambulance.

Despite the pain and fear, I still went to the retreat. Weeks later, I was still in significant pain, so I sought five medical opinions, all affirming that I needed surgery. According to the doctors, my L4-L5 disc had bulged out of my spine. I could not move, lift, bend, or run without tremendous pain; I could barely walk. Eventually, I agreed to the Laminectomy surgery with the hope that it would alleviate my pain even though I was terrified because it was my first major surgery. I was under the knife for about four or five hours, and when I woke up, my wife and mother were at my bedside. The months of recovery, while both in the hospital and out, was notably painful.

I was in the hospital for six days for recovery, and while there, I was on a pump for morphine pain medication. The nurse told me to squeeze the pump whenever I felt pain. The morphine medication would make me feel better, just as fast as the sleep aids would knock me out in college. The medication didn't provide just physical relief—there was a mental component to it as well. It had a total relaxing effect that made me feel like I was on top of the world, laying in the hospital bed, full of morphine, on the phone, calling anyone who would answer, just to say "hello." Despite this friendly and euphoric high the medication would give me, the scary part was that I went from activating the pump every two to three minutes to every five seconds.

When I was released from the hospital, my medical team prescribed me pills to manage the pain. I took the medication every four to six hours as prescribed, and then I eventually increased dosage to every one to two hours. The more I swallowed, the more my tolerance level increased. Before long, two pills would not get the job done, so I required more medication to reach the desired effect that I was used to. I was unconsciously becoming addicted at this point. I wasn't just using the pills for pain management, but I began taking the pills to psychologically cope with life. Physical and emotional dependence can occur with ongoing use of mood-altering substances, even when taken as directed by the practitioner.

First Signs of My Opioid Use Disorder

The opioid substance use changed my behavior and turned me into another person. Particular areas of the brain control our sense of pleasure and reward; scoring a shot during a basketball game, getting a promotion, or eating your favorite dessert are examples of things that cause dopamine to be released from the brain to give your body a rush. With opioid usage, the same thing happens, except your brain is instead *flooded* with dopamine, giving you an indescribable high. Over time, these parts of your brain become rewired, and you soon become unable to experience pleasure as you did before using opioids.

In addition to the chemical alterations in my brain, the pills became a central presence in my life—everything else revolved around my relationship with the pills.

When I had my pain medication, everything was okay, and when I didn't, I felt horrible and became anxious, loud, and angry, often verbally and emotionally abusing my wife. I said things that hurt her very deeply and that I regret to this day. It was confusing because I'm sure my behavior seemingly came out of nowhere and was inconsistent. With each new day, there was never any telling how I would act, and furthermore, my mood would often switch in the middle of the evening. Crystal withstood it for as long as she could, but eventually, she left and went back to Texas.

I was frustrated about her departure, but I was surprisingly not devastated. If anything, I saw the separation as an opportunity for more time and space to deepen my relationship with both the pills and the church. I could use without being questioned by my wife; I could get irritated and not have to worry about offending anyone at home; I could spend as much time in the church as I wanted without feeling guilty about being away from the family too long. That did not mean I had a good-riddance attitude, but I was a surely bit cocky. In my mind, I would do what I needed to do in this transitional period of time then simply get my family back.

Then something happened without my involvement: my wife had a baby shower with her family in Texas during our separation. Then shortly after that shower, about 40 women from our church in Corona flew to Texas on their own dime to surprise her with *another* baby shower. I realized that this gesture was a pure expression of how much they loved her and wanted her to come back. The effort clearly meant a lot to her because after four months of being away, she and our two sons finally came back home.

Upon her return, I attempted to be more responsible: we put in the work to buy a new house, which we were both excited about. It was practically brand new and felt like a much-needed fresh start, but I quickly realized that no matter where you go, *you* follow *you.* You can change locations, but the character stays within you. The change was good for our marriage at first, but after several months, things went back to how they were. Everything that had not been fixed met us right there in the new house, which included my addiction and all the hell that came with it.

PRE-CONTEMPLATION

———◆———

"I feel that as long as you're honest, you have the opportunity to grow. It's when you shut down, go into denial, and try to start hiding things from yourself and others, that's when you lock in certain behaviors and attitudes that keep you stuck."

—Tracy McMillan, author of the blog
"Why You're Not Married"

Living in Denial

Eventually, the pain from my back surgery subsided, but the pill-popping routine was already in full effect. Without my medication, I began experiencing withdrawal symptoms: vomiting, shakes, sweats, constipation, restless legs, and hot and cold flashes. I also was not sleeping, which only heightened my short temper. There was no confusion though; I knew what I needed—another prescription.

When I was in sixth grade, I was covering first base when I got hit with a baseball, cracking my two front teeth. My teammate's dad was a dentist, so he quickly readjusted my teeth which held steady until arriving at the dentist. Years later, as an adult, months after my back surgery, I'd go to the doctor's and use my tooth excuse to get a medication refill. They would do an x-ray on my teeth and see that I had two previous root canals; I'd then get a refill and have 30 more days. By this point, I was dependent on the opioids with no full knowledge or real concern for the repercussions.

If ever I needed to be around people or felt that I needed to "perform," I would make sure that I had pills in my system. The problem was that my ministerial vocation called for me to be in front of people often, so I popped pills routinely—two to three tablets every three hours. Like clockwork, I was strategically consuming pain medication at 6 a.m., 9 a.m., noon, 3 p.m., 6 p.m., 9 p.m., and then again at midnight. I even drove under the influence, not knowing the severity of having opioids in my system. Thankfully, I never got a DUI, possession charge, or worse, I never physically hurt or killed someone while driving.

I used before church. I would take some before arriving then again about 10 minutes right before my sermons to avoid withdrawals while at the podium. If I started withdrawing while preaching, I always had two pills in the pulpit absorbed in grape soda. Opioids induce hyperhidrosis—excessive sweating—which can be uncomfortable and embarrassing. I would put wash rags in my armpits to absorb some of the sweat, but inside my suit, it was like waterfalls. If I started to experience withdraws in front of people, I would pretend to cough and slide a pill in my mouth. I didn't even need to wait for it to dissolve in my bloodstream to feel better—just knowing that it was in my system gave me a boost. When I started losing weight due to lack of appetite, I'd tell inquisitive church members that I was simply exercising.

A description of the pre-contemplation stage of change is the point in addiction when the abuser has no intention of changing their behavior for the foreseeable future. The substance abuser may not even think they have a problem, and like me, they may be perfectly content with his or her habit. In this stage, the person says things such as, "I've got it under control," "It's not that bad," or, "I don't have an addiction problem." Unless a person is willing to realize that he or she might have an addiction problem, a person in pre-contemplation is unapproachable, particularly on subjects related to abuse or addiction.

Looking back, I realized that I used for four main reasons:

1. **I started using out of curiosity.** Similar to when I was in college and wanted to see what the sleep aids would do, I used the morphine in the hospital after my back surgery for the same reason: to simply find out how it would make me feel.

2. **I wanted to feel good.** Like most substance abusers, I was chasing the euphoria, the high. I liked how it felt to be on cloud nine, and I wanted to be there as often as possible.

3. **I wanted to feel better.** It wasn't always about getting high. The pills made me feel physically normal and without pain after a while. Without them, I experienced severe withdrawals, so I was also using just to get back that normal feeling again.

4. **I wanted to perform better.** I felt that when I was under the influence, I preached better and interacted better with people in general.

Whenever I listen to old sermons of mine, I hear how slurred my speech was. It was clear that I was in denial at the time of using, and having a prescription deterred me from thinking I had a problem. Eventually, I ceased experiencing euphoria— the medicine didn't have the same effect on me. By then, I was just trying to feel normal because without the pills, I had the shakes and the sweats, and not to mention, I was also hell to deal with; I was not a pleasant person to be around when I was sober. Unfortunately, I took a lot of my frustrations out on my wife.

I was never physically abusive with Crystal, but I was verbally and emotionally harmful. I will forever regret my behavior towards her. She could not identify the source of my issue or my anger, but she was plenty aware that something was wrong. When I was taking my pills regularly and by schedule, I was a great person to be around. She would say things like, "Man, you seem happy today." I would say, "Yeah, baby. I'm doing extraordinarily good." When either the medication wore off or I was out of pills, I would immediately dwindle down to feeling and behaving terribly. I became erratic and out of control.

Flagged

I maintained my pill acquisition routine without interruption until the doctors caught on and flagged me. To help combat the growing epidemic of opioid abuse and the over-prescribing of them, many US states use a Prescription Monitoring Program (PMP) or Prescription Drug Monitoring Program (PDMP) to provide practitioners and pharmacists with digital access to a patient's history of dispensed controlled substance prescriptions. If an individual is getting too many prescriptions in too short of a time period, the record will be flagged.

Since my record was flagged, I was denied more pain medication from the doctor and pharmacy, so I started buying it off the street; I began chasing the high at all costs. I needed it and couldn't function without it. Over time, opioids take on an abnormally high priority. Your sole aim from the moment you rise out of bed is to get, consume, and experience the drug at the expense of things we would otherwise hold at absolute value, including relationships. It hijacks your brain and your life and ultimately leads to self-destruction.

Dr. Carlo DiClemente, a professor at the University System of Maryland, who specializes in addiction and health behavior change, listed four reasons why people end up in the pre-contemplation stage. These reasons are considered "the Four R's":

▶ **Reluctant** pre-contemplators don't fully know the depth of their problem or the personal impact it can have for them to think they need to change. Alternatively, they also don't have the desire to change due to inertia, stemming from certain beliefs, attitudes, thought patterns, and life habits. These factors keep them stagnant.

▶ **Rebellious** pre-contemplators have a heavy investment in their substance of choice as well as being in control of their own lives. They don't like being told to change or what to do.

▶ **Resigned** pre-contemplators are overwhelmed by the problems caused by the addiction and are scared at the thought of going without their substance of choice. Many have attempted to quit in the past but are now hopeless about the possibility of change.

▶ **Rationalizing** pre-contemplators have plenty of reasons (i.e., excuses) as to why their substance of choice is not a problem or why it's a problem for others but not for them.

I learned that I can be quite rebellious, but there was no doubt that I identified most as a reluctant pre-contemplator, believing that I was not a drug abuser because I was using prescription pills versus common street drugs. My unfamiliarity with the opioid epidemic played an enormous role in my hesitance to abandon the pain pills. Moreover, as I continued to consume and abuse, my disorder grew and with good reason. According to the National Institute on Drug Abuse, prescription opioids behave similarly to heroin, attacking the very same brain systems.

Diagnosed

Certain drugs (opioids included) can trigger mental health issues, which was the case with me. In contrast, psychological issues can trigger substance use disorders. In some cases, mania, depression, anxiety, irritability, and insomnia persist after the drugs wear off, which can be an indication that a co-occurring mental health disorder is present. Paranoia and delusions were not specifically my symptoms, but depression paired with mania, irritability, and instability were. Those closest to me—my wife, my parents, and a church leader—convinced me for a good while to see a psychiatrist. I felt an obligation to go as opposed to wanting to go. I might not have known that I had a co-occurring disorder, but I certainly knew that I had a problem. I just wasn't ready to change.

Fortunately, I followed through with my word that I would see a psychiatrist. I cannot recall exactly how long it took from the time they asked me to go until the time I relented, but I was eventually diagnosed with bipolar disorder and prescribed psychotropic medication to keep me balanced. I felt relief in that I finally had a name for my imbalance, yet it was frustrating that I had a new burdensome label placed on me. Sometimes I would take my medication, and other times I would not, simply to avoid feeling as though I needed help.

I quickly realized that my thoughts, feelings, and behavior fell apart when I was not compliant with my medication. I struggled because I couldn't mix the psychotropic medication with the opioids, and accepting that something was wrong with me didn't help either. I knew I was not the only one in my world with mental health issues, but I assumed that very few people, especially church leaders, were dealing with similar issues. In retrospect, trying to hide it from everyone made it worse than it had to be. Back when my usage was a secret, it was out of control; now that I had help, it was manageable.

There are numerous reasons why substance abusers, including myself, do not want help—fear and shame headline the list. The negative stigma and discrimination associated with addiction are far from ideal. Ignorance, the blissful state of not knowing, is another. If you simply cannot see that you have a problem, then you simply do not think you need help. This was precisely my issue for a very long time; not being able to trust the therapist was another. Inability to trust can be especially true for those in leadership positions; fear of information coming out deters those individuals from simply not seeking help. External barriers, such as not having financial means to get help, can also be particularly unfortunate in cases where someone knows help is required and wants it but simply cannot afford it.

Any of these factors—external or internal—delay or obstruct appropriate care and can be a challenge to overcome. Further complicating matters, several of these issues may exist simultaneously. These additional hurdles are more prevalent among certain nationalities, genders, educational, and socioeconomic groups. It is crucial to remember, too, that it is a process; getting help does not mean that the situation will immediately turn around. It takes time.

While sitting in the psychiatrist's office, I knew I had no intention of quitting the pills. After being prescribed psychotropic medication to help with my bipolar disorder, I did not take them consistently. Changing myself was not my top priority at the time—using in peace and privacy was. Reducing the stigma and discrimination of asking for help and speaking openly about mental health issues requires constant and continuous efforts on all communicative fronts. Until a no-shame culture is created, people will always continue to suffer issues unnecessarily.

CONTEMPLATION

——◆——

*Insanity: doing the same thing over and over
and expecting different results."*

—Albert Einstein

Losing It All

Two church members—a man and a woman—pulled me to the side after worship service one Sunday and accused me of using drugs. The man, a leader of the church, was a law enforcement officer, and the woman was a faithful church member. Given his occupation as an officer, I'm sure the man recognized my behaviors—the signs—of an addict, which then led me to realize that I did not know how people viewed me. In my head, I conquered everything: I was in control, and I was not using illegal drugs. This man and woman's accusations were correct. I rationalized and justified their complaint because I was just taking prescription pills: "I don't know who told you that, but they are lying." I was defensive, adamant, and angered. If I knew where that man was today, I would apologize to him—he was right about me all along.

Once I hit the contemplation stage, I was four years into my addiction. I started realizing I had an issue. Personal acknowledgment and accountability are critical for making the first step towards improvement, and I finally arrived at that essential point in my journey. I quickly learned, however, that uncertainty and conflicting emotions began playing a role in this process. I started to refuse to believe my issue, but it had also gotten to the point that I could no longer deny it. Others around me, I'm sure, wanted to address me, but they were too afraid of me pushing them away. The inner conflict of wanting to get better and also living in denial added to the difficult recovery process. I continued using, even though I knew better, and as a result, I suffered the consequences.

I still wanted to change. I was not sure how to, and the thought of treatment, recovery, related expenses, detox, and the differing emotions scared me. Being exposed as an opioid user terrified me even more. I started weighing the pros and cons of seeking help and treatment and began making many resolutions, but until I made a final decision, I knew progress wouldn't happen. Those suffering from substance use disorders may stay in the contemplation stage until something drastic enough convinces them to get help, which is precisely what happened to me. It was still not an overnight occurrence—it was a process.

In the fall of 2008, my wife became fed up and left again. Her departure was the catalyst to really and truly turn my life around this time. That insight and gratitude live in the present, but at that time, her leaving made me furious. It was more than just being upset with her for leaving or at myself for messing up our marriage—I was disillusioned into feeling as though it was her fault for making me lose it all. When she left, she did not just take our union and our children with her—she tarnished my reputation; she snatched my influence as a preacher; she erased my career. She took everything.

The day she called to tell me she was leaving, I was driving home from one of my speaking engagements.

My ego refused to believe her, but my spirit knew better. Although I had not yet arrived at the house to confirm whether or not she had really left or if I had time to reconcile our differences, I decided to call my church leader at the time; I wanted guidance and comforting. I needed someone to give me a key or a magic word to tell my wife to make her come back home. Instead, he informed me in a calm yet firm voice, "You are done. Either resign with dignity, or you will be terminated."

In a matter of 24 hours, I lost my two biggest priorities: my family and my church. For a while, I was in denial. I went home that day to an empty house. I popped several pills before reality had a chance to set in. I wanted euphoria back because the second that sobriety emerged, so did the hurt, the disbelief, and the embarrassment. I was still less concerned with the fact that my family had left; somewhere in the back of my mind, I knew that I would see them again—even if it was only for the sake of the children. I knew, however, that the church was something that I could not get back; the minds of the church leaders could not be changed. My dream of ministering to a multicultural congregation that God and the people would be proud of was crushed.

Looking back, I do not blame the church for letting me go. I was emotionally unreliable. I was a liability that they could not afford to carry. They didn't know I was sick, so even if they wanted to help me, they couldn't since my pill addiction was kept a secret. I suffered my substance use disorder in silence, and then my life was taken from me. My career was gone; my identity was gone; my popularity was gone; my influence was gone; all those years of practice and preparation were gone.

Around this same time, a friend of mine died in a plane crash. His family asked me to preach his eulogy, which was also at the same California church that I would soon be leaving. His eulogy was my last sermon. It was remarkably emotional and difficult to execute for many reasons. My friend was gone, my life was crumbled, and I would likely never see the congregation again. Over the years with that church, I had baptized, counseled, and married many of the members; I buried their loved ones; I studied with them; the circumstances meant, however, that I would not be continuing with them. I saw myself as a failure and disappointment. I was heartbroken and began questioning if life needed me anymore.

On the Sunday after my friend's funeral and during my final sermon, I stood before the church with tears in my eyes and announced that I was leaving. I didn't want to disclose the details into why I was leaving or the fact that I was given an ultimatum to resign or be terminated; I didn't want to shame myself further or cause any discord in the church. I tried to keep the church together and in good spirits. Considering how good they had all been to me, it was the least I could do. Telling them I was leaving was the hardest message I have ever delivered.

I repented my drug usage, but this feeling of regret and remorse only lasted for two days. Quitting drugs is difficult, but in my case, opioids were especially challenging due to the euphoria they brought me. By this point, I was no longer in denial; I knew the pills were addictive and caused me and my life harm. I knew that I had to break my habit. It felt like I was living in a state of "damned if I do, damned if I don't." If I quit, I knew I was headed for severe mental and physical withdrawals: intense irritability, insomnia, night sweats, muscle aches, bodily cramps, constipation, nausea, and vomiting. I was in contract and contact with the Devil; it seemed as though He'd come to kill, steal, and destroy what little I had left.

After my two-day sacrifice, not only did I go back to using, but I increased my dosage. I needed to numb the pain and fill the emptiness in my broken soul, and nothing from prayer, exercising, or attending church seemed to help. Withdrawals only made it worse, so I threw my hands up in the air and gave up. I simply didn't care anymore. My attitude became: "it is what it is, it ain't what it ain't, it's gonna be what it's gonna be." The deeper I drowned in my struggle, the stronger the resentment towards my wife became. Looking back, her departure was to everyone's benefit. Had she not gone, we would not be married today.

About a month after she left, I decided to go to her. Before relocating back to Texas, I attempted to short sale our California house, but I could not, and it ended up going into foreclosure. What I thought was the worst was turning into devastating. Every corner I turned, there seemed to be more bad news awaiting me. I was done living in California, so I moved back to Texas to live with my grandmother.

Feeling hypocritical and abandoned by God, I left the ministry for over a six or seven-month period. I didn't practice preaching and rarely attended church. A voice in my head kept saying, "Son, I created you. I love you. It is not over. I'm still shaping you. I'm not through with you. I'm with you. You will smile again. You will laugh again. I'm walking with you. I will never leave you nor forsake you." This voice was the sole point of encouragement that kept me going. The few times I did go to church, I would sneak in and sit in the back pew and listen to the singing and preaching while swallowing pills at the same time. I was silently deteriorating and battling for my life in that seat; I attended with the hope of hearing something that might help me. I so desperately wanted to be restored, healed, and forgiven, yet I would still sneak in and right back out just to avoid interaction and conversations. The Devil had me, and it was as though I never stepped foot in the sanctuary. I started barbering again, slowly gaining enough clients to make ends meet and somewhat get back on my feet. I was also still buying pills off the streets.

What I failed to realize at the time was that I was a masterpiece statue hidden within an uncarved stone

Breaking Down

In order for God to rebuild me, I had to be broken down and humbled first. I remember calling Crystal with tears in my eyes one day, apologizing for everything I had done and hadn't done. I confessed that I wanted to take my life and asked her to tell our children that I loved them dearly. I had a bottle of alcohol in my hand and meant every word about giving up. Twenty minutes later, my father showed up. He put his arms around me, hugging me, not letting me go. I feel, to this day, that God sent him to save my life by holding me like the day I was born.

Two weeks later, my wife called, wanting me to come back home, which was the very moment of conception of our reconciliation. I was blessed with yet another chance to be with my wife. My wife and children got an apartment in Texas and did our best to make it work. She was teaching at school, and I was cutting hair. After a few months of this lifestyle, she convinced me to get back into preaching. I reluctantly agreed and was invited by a small church to become their preacher. The problem was that I was still using and was still in a pretty poor condition.

When Crystal became pregnant with our third child, I was pumped; not only was another child coming into our world, but I knew she would have another Caesarean section—which meant that she would be prescribed opioids. I quickly got into the rhythm of swapping some regular ibuprofen with her pain pills; she could not tell the difference. When she needed the prescription, I eagerly volunteered to get them for her—and made sure to get myself a few in the process.

PREPARATION

---◆---

"If you can't fly then run, if you can't run then walk, if you can't walk then crawl, but whatever you do you have to keep moving forward."

—Dr. Martin Luther King Jr.

Meeting Rock Bottom

After hitting rock bottom, the substance abuser begins to prepare for recovery. In this stage, he identifies goals, objectives, and plans, making firm resolutions to cease the behavior once and for all. This phase showcases the user's determination to push forward and never return to the place of addiction. For example, people with alcohol addiction might consume beer instead of liquor, mistakenly thinking that reducing the severity of intake would mean higher hopes of total abstinence. At this stage, the substance abuser may experience fear at envisioning life without the drug that carried them for years.

While driving south on Interstate 35 in Dallas one day, I decided to call my wife's uncle who could relate to this demon. He was the only person at that point who I had completely opened up to. During this phone call, I told him everything, and it was the first time I told the truth about my illness. I had previously opened up to my wife when reconciling to admit and apologize for how I had treated her, but I had not fully and completely disclosed my battle with prescription drugs.

My wife's uncle was in recovery as well, so I knew he would understand and be less likely to judge me. Before this moment of self-disclosure, I thought rock bottom was leaving California, but it was not. It was when I picked up the phone to call him that I realized I was dying a slow death with nowhere else to go. I was physically, mentally, emotionally, and spiritually lost. I had already reached the point where I contemplated taking my own life because I was deteriorating so fast. I simply did not know if this life was for me anymore. So I prayed and asked God, "Is this it for me? Because if this is not, I don't know if there is any point of me being here anymore." When you lose everything that you have worked so hard for, the ground begins to crumble beneath your feet. I was losing my footing with nothing to cling to, drowning in a state of chronic depression.

I went to see a psychiatrist; they put me on Suboxone, which helped me transition from the opium by curbing the withdrawals. They did not tell me, however, how addictive it was. Suboxone contains buprenorphine, a low-level opiate designed to ironically cut opiate withdrawal symptoms. Taking Suboxone was just as hard, if not harder, to get off of. I battled with that substance for about a year, and since I was paying out of pocket, this addiction was costly.

I was miserable, feeling like the prodigal son in the pigpen and the apostle Paul chained in the midnight hour. I felt alone and lifeless—existing but not living. I thought I had nowhere else to go. I was back with my family and attending church again, but my heart was in a faraway place, far from the cross and in the streets.

I felt like the living dead. When I was in church, dressed, suited, and looking good, the drugs consumed my heart, and my heart was consumed by the drugs. I wanted out, but I was hitting walls everywhere I went. I even failed treatment.

ACTION

---◆---

"What lies behind us and what lies before us are tiny matters compared to what lies within us."

—Ralph Waldo Emerson, author

The Prodigal Son

I was sitting in my church office one day with the door closed, and I was experiencing severe withdrawals. I locked the door out of fear; I was unsure of what was about to happen to me. I was sweating, shaking, and feeling like I was right on top of death. This episode was ten times worse than the flu. The only treatment I had on me was the Suboxone, which was the very thing that was causing me to suffer.

In the action stage, the substance abuser will begin taking immediate action towards his recovery and success. He or she may attend an inpatient addiction treatment program and follow a continuum of care afterward. Substance abusers also learn how their illness prohibits a healthy lifestyle. They have also regained hope in their ability to change and have accepted that turning their lives around meant a canceled relationship with their drug of choice.

I declared then, right there in that office, that I was stopping once and for all. I was disgusted with myself, sitting in a church going through withdrawals. No one in the congregation knew my struggle. Although I was no longer using Suboxone, I was still hiding the fact that I was trying to recover from my substance use disorder.

I didn't want people to witness any of my unexplained bodily movements or sweats, so when it came time for me to preach, I would not arrive at the pulpit until the exact moment I was due. I had a suit on, so it helped to camouflage these physical signs; you would have never been able to tell. I was clean: shiny suit, shoes, and Bible. I was making folks laugh, but inside I was battling. Finally, on that day on the couch in my office, I just said to myself, "you know what, I'm going to quit," and I remember the prayer that I verbalized.

It was a prayer I had never recited: I was requesting God's hand to reach down and touch me. It wasn't like a prayer I would pronounce in front of the church using big fancy religious words; this was the most intimate and heartfelt moment of my life. I recall the Lord asking Saul of Tarsus, "Why are you persecuting me?" I felt like Jesus was saying to me, "Brandon, why are you doing this to yourself? I need you back in the pulpit, but more importantly, leading your wife and children." It was then, at that moment, that I asked for deliverance. Clinically, there are multiple opinions on how to enter sustained sobriety, but for me, I had to first reconnect spiritually with my Creator. I begged God various times to remove the thorn of addiction out of my flesh. I was sitting in the church as a preacher with no one to preach to me and nowhere to go.

That day in my office, the action stage started, and I stopped the Suboxone cold turkey. It was a stupid thing to do. I should have consulted with my psychiatrist first; my resulting withdrawal symptoms lasted for about four months. Simply put, the longer you abuse, the longer you withdraw. There were times when I considered going back to the pills simply because the process was so painful and miserable, but I stayed the course. I knew that if I returned to the crutch of the drug, I might never make it out alive. I had already decided that enough was enough—I was tired of being sick and tired, and it was time to move forward. I had to fight, push, and conquer. That was the ultimate challenge. When you first stop taking a drug, the first few days to weeks (depending on the person and length of use) of the physiological fight is the most intense. If you can fight through the initial few days or weeks and physically get it out of your system, the physiological withdraws turn to psychological.

Everyone responds to these symptoms and processes differently, but the physical withdrawals do not typically last nearly as long as the psychological. Let's say, for instance, that I stopped using for two days. Mentally, I'll tell myself that I have to start using again because I feel physically sick, which describes the physiological and psychological symptoms occurring simultaneously.

I promised the Lord, "If you get me off of this, I promise you: I will never voluntarily ingest mood-altering addictive substances again." I'm not saying the Lord took me off of the pills right then and there because I still had to make daily choices myself to stay sober. When the

Lord shifts you into a new dimension, He will provide multiple options available to you.

In the past, I would quit several times for two to three days but always relapsed. This time was different; I knew if I returned to drug use, I would face an institution, jail, or even death. My life was on the line, and the withdrawals I went through were terrible enough to truly say, "never again."

Since that day on the church couch, I stayed the course, remained focused, and continued to tell myself that there was hope. I also finally told my wife the truth—that I was battling for my life every day. With time, patience, and dedication, the withdrawals got better. I thank God daily.

MAINTENANCE

---◆---

"I hated every minute of training, but I said, 'Don't quit. Suffer now and live the rest of your life as a champion.'"

—Muhammad Ali, boxing heavyweight champ, inspirational leader, innovator, and icon

Expanding My Word

Three months had gone by, and things were turning around for my family and me. I was off the Suboxone. Crystal and I still had our marriage challenges, but things between us were getting better. It was as though God was opening up doors for me; my father's college roommate invited me to assume a full-time preaching position at his church. I accepted and moved the family to Baytown, Texas.

In addition to the new position, my friend and assistant minister Terrell Williams and I decided to attend the Institute of Chemical Dependency Studies in Houston, TX. We were determined to obtain licensure, so this drug counseling school prepared us to become Licensed Chemical Dependency Counselors. I dreaded the first day of class, fearing the teacher would ask us if we were in recovery, which would expose my truth to my assistant minister. I was not ready for that. I realized I was in post-recovery pre-contemplation; the substance abuse was over, but I still held onto the secret. At the very beginning of class, the instructor did indeed ask, "Who is in recovery?" Of course, I lied and denied. Towards the end of the program, we had a female guest presenter named of Ms. Carol J. Nunn who demonstrated a masterful presentation on "Motivational Interviewing." She directed a treatment

program in the Texas state jail and was very knowl-
edgeable in the field of chemical dependency and had
a 15-year tenure with her company. At the conclusion
of her presentation, she offered the students help in
finding internship availabilities. Because of her expert
knowledge and my determination, I had already decided that I wanted to work for her. I called and emailed
her weekly, probably getting on her nerves, waiting for
my criminal background approval so I could begin
counseling in the state jail. She eventually hired me under her supervision and the supervision of the assistant
director, Toby Bradley. I completed a 240-hour practi-
cum and began the rigorous 4,000-hour internship at
the state jail. During the internship, I passed the state
exam. On September 19, 2016, upon completing the
hours, I officially became a Licensed Chemical Dependency Counselor (LCDC).

The coverup of my truth was still weighing heav-
ily on my heart, so I sat down with my director one
day and confessed with an apology: "I was not honest
with you when I interviewed; I lied to you. I struggled
with opioids for years." She responded with, "I know.
I have been doing this for 20 years—I knew you were
lying when you said it." She encouraged me to always
remain true and honest with myself. She raised a point:
"If you really want to be an effective pastor, consider
praying about whether you should share your testimo-
ny and you make the choice. Otherwise, you're really

not genuinely preaching—you're just reading scriptures and telling stories. In my mind, I was thinking that admitting my past could translate into losing my job at the church. Just watch the response you get." I felt like a freight train was about to hit me. Throughout a twenty-year history of preaching, I finally had an eye-opening moment. It was time to reveal my truth.

Nervous wasn't the word. I was terrified, but I was committed to following through. I compiled a sermon called "Breaking the Chains of Chemical Dependency." I used Noah, a man of God and builder of the ark, as my example. The Bible is not clear if Noah had an alcohol use disorder, but it's possible through hints of scripture and behavior patterns; the world then was a sinful environment. Regardless, Noah was appointed to construct a boat, and he was on the boat for 40 days with family and animals. Noah was a husband, father, preacher, captain, and possibly a veterinarian simultaneously; I can sense and relate to the pressure he may have experienced. It was possible that he had no way to cope with everything he had been through, so he built an altar then a grape vineyard. He then drank to intoxication and was naked and exposed. I shared with the church, "I can relate to Noah today. Just like Noah was a man of God who battled with and experienced substance abuse, I did too." That sermon was my entrance into a new level of ministry. After testifying in front of all those people, it instantly felt like a five thousand-pound concrete burden, years of secrecy, manipulation, lies, deceit, anger, pain, and hurt had resurrected off my back. My truth had finally set me free.

So many wonderful people from the pulpit expressed gratitude for my self-disclosure that day. Tears of joy rolled down my cheeks as church members shared their direct and indirect history with all sorts of addiction. One specific person said her respect level for me shifted to an all-time high because she knew her preacher was authentic, transparent, human, and honest. Ever since that day, I have not been ashamed to talk about my co-occurring disorders. I continue to grow with my family daily. We have since been blessed with a beautiful baby girl named Harper. I have been blessed with the ability to preach every Sunday for the amazing multicultural Connect Church that God placed in my life in 2016 as well as the honor to counsel others in the Texas jail system as an LCDC.

These days, I feel very healthy, mentally sound, and thankful that God carried me through the storm until I was strong enough to walk on my own. I can accurately admit that "I don't look like what I've been through, but I will never forget." I absolutely had to go through that struggle, and when I look back over it now, I realize today that God never abandoned me—I left Him. I no longer preach or counsel to impress, to sound good or look good. My new life's mission is to motivate and inspire people to uncover their truth and be free.

It wasn't until about four years ago that I became completely comfortable speaking my truth; I will always have an addictive personality, and any person, place, or thing can trigger a relapse. A substance use disorder will forever reside within me; I simply had to accept that.

The most crucial stage of upkeep, even after treatment and regardless to what the addiction might be, is maintaining health and preventing relapse. Maintaining recovery requires focusing and implementing the tools learned in treatment—being active in recovery programs, building support groups, and living life without the temptation to use. Once I got to a place where I was away from the opioids, it has not been an issue since. I know today that if I relapse, I may not return back to recovery. When people relapse, it's common for them to use the same amount of drugs before entering recovery, but because their bodies can't handle the amount after being without the substance for a certain period of time, it often results in overdose.

I was a functional user, taking maybe five to ten pills a day. If I took even one pill, then, it would trigger a downhill relapse, and I never want to relive that period of withdrawal again and the corresponding feeling I had when I came home and my family had left me. At first, I was resentful towards my wife because I felt she made me lose my job at the church. She knew that congregation meant a lot to me, and she knew I was really upset at her since I felt she took that from underneath my feet. In all reality, however, I think I was so interested and concerned with the church that I wasn't paying attention at ministering to my family—my number one ministry.

As a minister, your first ministry obligation is to your family—not the congregation—so when she left me, I wasn't mad that she left; I was mad that I lost my job at the church. I saw that she was the reason because of that. She didn't try to talk to me; she just left. When we were in the process of divorcing, the papers were already started, and funny enough, our lawyers happened to be working on a case with two people with the same names as us, Brandon and Crystal. That's precisely when we said to each other, "you know what—maybe God is trying to keep us together."

Things are better now, but emotionally abandoning my family was one of my biggest regrets, not church. "To thy own self be true." I was finally honest with myself. You can't be honest with anybody until you are honest with yourself. I had to say to myself, "I have an opioid use disorder." Not *had*; I *have* one. Today I say, I will never be recovered but always in recovery.

I eventually came to realize that I'm the one who lost the church—the church did not leave me. My choices and behavior led to my loss of employment.

Crystal didn't leave me as a person; she left my behavior. My resentment towards her lasted probably for two or three years after that because I lost a great financial situation and had to start all over again. I was contemplating divorce because I felt Crystal had taken it all from me, and the way she did it while I was away only heightened my infuriation. But when I look back on it now, I realize it had to happen.

If it didn't happen, I would be in prison or dead. This realization inspired me to contact the California church leaders via mail, apologizing and asking them to forgive me. I confessed everything, which took quite a long time to do because back then, they had tried to help me. I give them "much kudos"—they were trying to help me with a total behavior change. I then followed up with a phone call and verbally apologized. I told the leadership how sorry I was for bringing shame upon the church, not being able to last as their preacher, and how apologetic and remorseful I was. It took a lot of humility for me to do that, but that was when God met me in the midnight hour and helped me transition onto the road to recovery.

God gave me so many more opportunities in life, and today I have a greater appreciation for what He's given me now. There is no shame in my past or my present. I am who I am. You are who you are. You are awesome. You are destined for greatness. You are a star. Be happy about who you are. Everyone struggles with something. Nobody's perfect. Keep striving. Keep fighting. Keep pushing. Keep believing. Do not let your past hinder you. Reach your destiny, but learn the lessons on the road.

I've been sober for nine years now, and just as I promised God, I never put any more addictive substances into my system again. My relationship with God continues to grow daily, and I'm in a different place in life now. I never want to go back to that world of addiction, as I am very family and career-oriented. I have a purpose to serve God and humanity. I'm giving back to my brothers and sisters in the pews, the prison, the streets, society, and to those who are currently fighting the fight. I feel compelled to fight for those I'm trying to help and those who can't fight for themselves.

CONCLUSION

You never know how strong you are until you have to be. Hitting rock bottom is painful in every way imaginable—emotionally, mentally, physically, spiritually, and financially. Reaching this point leaves you with no choice but to confront yourself and your demons. That confrontation will be brutal and honest yet necessary. There is no going around hurtful moments, bad habits, and hang-ups—you simply must go through it. Character, integrity, and strength are constantly tested in the storms of life.

One of the hardest realizations I had to face was that my opioid use disorder was only one layer to my addiction. It was rooted in something much deeper—a need for approval, to be loved, to be admired, and to be accepted. Had I never realized this, other addictions would have taken the place of the opioids, and I would have never regained my sense of peace and fulfillment. Something would have always been missing, despite having everything I could need to not only survive but thrive.

Rock bottom has the power to reveal all of your dysfunctional behaviors. It holds a mirror up to your face, giving you the chance to finally look yourself in the eyes and make a choice to save yourself or drown. If you never reach this moment of truth, the dysfunctions continue unnoticed and unchecked while you waddle in denial, inevitably creating bigger dysfunctions. Until you drop all the balls, you cleverly deceive yourself into believing that you're juggling just fine and everything's great, even when it's not.

Your self-destructive patterns become glaringly obvious, and the triggers that kept you repeating those cycles come into sharp focus when you're at your lowest. Fortunately, I realized that hitting rock bottom was not only inevitable but critical because there's no other way to change or grow. Looking back, I understand how insane those cycles were—constantly creating the same dynamics and keeping the drama alive, playing the same role, and wondering why nothing was ever enough. It's not until you break the mold and start the journey back to your true self that you stop playing those broken records and begin designing new realities.

As crazy as it sounds, I look back on my secret battle with immense gratitude for the many lessons and blessings bestowed upon me during that time of tribulation. It instilled an even deeper trust that God had and has my back—through thick and thin—contrary to what the external circumstances looked and felt like. That acknowledgment granted me a level of confidence that I'd never before experienced. Once upon a time, I relied on external sources—my pills—to make me happy. Now, instead of relying on that outside validation, I trust myself, my unique life's journey, and my relationship with God. Facing my problems instead of continuing to run from them (or hide in them) presented me with a more meaningful life.

Whereas I was once ashamed of my addiction, I am thankful for the lessons learned, and I no longer try to hide my story. My truth set me free. This freedom was not immediate or always gratifying, but coming clean was definitely worth it. I emerged from the ashes more humble, more compassionate, more courageous, and far more grateful. Surviving my journey made me a better husband, father, church leader, and man of God. If you're currently battling secrets, I encourage you not to give up on yourself and to trust your Spirit through your darkest moments.

Your ability to soar, I've learned, is dependent upon your willingness to face your version of rock bottom. Don't give up, as you were born to bounce back. When you are willing to explore your darkest depths, you are truly ready to be of service in the world. The old foundations must crumble first, however, before you can begin rebuilding on new and solid ground. Maya Angelou, well-known poet and award-winning author, once stated (and I couldn't agree more) that, "I have great respect for the past. If you don't know where you've come from, you don't know where you are going. I have respect for the past, but I'm a person of the moment. I'm here, and I do my best to be completely centered at the place I'm at, then I go forward to the next place."

ABOUT THE AUTHOR

Nationally acclaimed minister, motivator, and counselor, Brandon Holt, LCDC, is a tour de force for our times. Dubbed "The People's Preacher," he came of age in the church in Arlington, Texas. He attended Williams Barber College, Southwestern Christian College, and the Institute of Chemical Dependency Studies. Today, he's a Licensed Chemical Dependency Counselor in Houston, Texas where he's doing the critical work of changing lives. Passionate about ministry, the tireless advocate planted the Connect Church of Christ in Baytown, Texas where he preaches weekly, empowering people to discover their truth in the inspired Word of God. Brandon and his wife, Crystal, have three boys and one daughter. He lives by his favorite personal mantra, "One day at a time."

To connect, visit his website at
www.brandonholt.org

CREATING DISTINCTIVE BOOKS
WITH INTENTIONAL RESULTS

We're a collaborative group of creative masterminds
with a mission to produce high-quality books to position
you for monumental success in the marketplace.

Our professional team of writers, editors, designers,
and marketing strategists work closely together to ensure
that every detail of your book is a clear representation
of the message in your writing.

Want to know more?
Write to us at info@publishyourgift.com
or call (888) 949-6228

Discover great books, exclusive offers, and more at
www.PublishYourGift.com

Connect with us on social media

@publishyourgift

CPSIA information can be obtained
at www.ICGtesting.com
Printed in the USA
LVOW13*2058090518
576647LV00002B/3/P

To:
Patrick John
God Bless

5-27-18